We Start With What We're Given

We Start With What We're Given

Poems by

Miriam O'Neal

Kelsay Books

© 2018 Miriam O'Neal. All rights reserved. This material may not be reproduced in any form, published, reprinted, recorded, performed, broadcast, without the express written consent of Miriam O'Neal. All such actions are strictly prohibited by law.

Cover design Shay Culligan
Cover photo: "Three Cornered Pond at Sunrise"
    by Miriam O'Neal

ISBN: 978-1-947465-91-6

Kelsay Books
Aldrich Press
www.kelsaybooks.com

Acknowledgements

Thank you to the editors of the following journals, where some of these poems appeared in earlier forms:

AGNI: "When You Ask Again"
Blackbird Journal: "Delivered"
Muddy River Review: "Kovno Ghetto, April 1942: Portrait Before Shabbat"
Nottingham Review: "Lesson 3—Distance"
Sierra Nevada Review: "Kovno Ghetto, March 1942: Imagining Mama's Birthday"
Solidago Journal: "I Imagine My Father Tries His Hand At Memoir, Again" and "Picasso's Women"
Solstice Literary Magazine: "March 3, 1991"
Temper: "We Start With What We're Given"

With gratitude to my parents, who gave me words, my husband, who gave me space, and my sons, who showed me how to trust the process.

Also, to Dvzinia Orlowsky, Mary Kane, Barbara Siegel Carlson, and Anne Doolittle, for their close reading of the work in progress. To my sisters, Meg and Lee, thank you for believing in me. I also owe much to the life and strength of artist Esther Lurie, whose art-making sustained her through the years of the Shoa and affirmed the place of art in preserving our humanity.

Contents

I

Delivered	11
Morning	12
Using the Dark	13
After Reading Cattafi's "Descent to the Throne"	14
Poise	16
Speaking of The Dead	17
My Mother Breaks Her Arm Sliding Down the Stairs on A Mattress	18
The Lady from the Choir Says, *Your Mother Was A Saint*	19
The Space In Between	21
The Blessing	22
Keeping Up	23
March 3, 1991	24
I Imagine My Father Tries His Hand at Memoir	25
Blue Swans	26
We Start With What We're Given	27
Song	29
Woolgathering	30

II

Translating Rilke In Winter	33
Lesson 1—Action	34
Picasso's Women	35
Upon Discovering the Task Is Larger Than First Predicted	36
This is a poem	37
Lesson 2—On Time and Desire	38

I Imagine My Father Tries His Hand at Memoir, Again	39
Shell Life	42
Poem	43
When You Ask Again	44
Why We Need Salt	45
Bread—1	46
Lesson 3—Distance	47
Morning Prayer	49

III

Kovno, 1939	53
Notes on "Girl with Yellow Star"	54
Kovno Ghetto, July 1941	55
Visitation	56
Kovno Ghetto, November 1941	58
Plymouth, October 2016	60
Kovno Ghetto, March 1942, Imagining Mamma's Birthday	61
Kovno Ghetto, April 1942, Portrait Before Shabbat Kovno Quotidian	63
Kovno Ghetto, January 1943	64
Kovno Ghetto, Spring 1943	65
Kovno Ghetto, June 1944	66
Kovno Ghetto, July 1944	67
Transport, July 1944	68
Plymouth, February 2017	69
Stutthof, 1944, Bread 2	70
Leibisch, August 1944, Nummer Schreiberen	71
Leibisch, October 1944	73
Tel Aviv, July 1945	75

Notes
About the Author

I

*Now I cannot remember if it was this life or some other,
if the color of the trees was indeed yellow. I cannot say for certain
that the light was retreating, whose death we were just then*

forgetting....

"November" by Mary Kane

Delivered

The little creek
its mossy shoulders,
fox scat—metallic green beetles
in black thumb-lengths of dung.
Cracked freshwater clamshells,
flecks of moon.
Birds stirring in the close brush.

Sky fills the sylph of water
the way a child fills its mother up
until she becomes simply
vessel—bears down like night on a mirror.

Eyes collect each particle of light.
The mind assembles—wraps
itself in the odor of cold water,
in laughter lugged from each little current.
All of it cocooned in a pocket
of a woods.

Before the nurse swaddled me
I lay trembling—
an icy creek a boot-clad girl had splashed
through, her eyes fixed on the far side.

Morning

In those days I never woke
from a dream of falling. The earth
was easy to leave and return to.

I climbed rocks along the beach
and leapt across the air,
one boulder to another,

left this world a dozen times a day,
returned through the portal of sound.

Waves sluiced jetties, gulls *sca-reeed*,
the lobster boats' engines *wumped*
just off shore.
So easy to be

there   not there   there,
to come and go without fear of falling
in either world,

carry the news
of each place inside me

the way a girl carries her eggs,
unfertilized,

filled with possibility.

Using the Dark

First, one child hid.
That was the basis of the game
played at dusk.

She found her place.
And when a seeker neared,
she beckoned, *Come to me*.

And those two hid
together, moved together
if need be, to another space

as one by one seekers
became hiders, crouched like stumps
or standing in shadows

like a grove of little trees
—using the dark,
the object to not be, the last seeker

left
in the failing light.

After Reading Cattafi's "Descent to the Throne"

A woman sits at the top of the stairs.
I'm not stopping to think it over,
how, as poems allow, I am beside her.

Skirts spread like collapsed tents,
buried from the waist down
we're gathering strength.

Her husband stands below us by the door,
mud on his shoes. *Before undertaking*
the descent to the throne

and squandering everything
he must bury the dead child.
And then I see my mother

in the thick of a summer
night in the early '60s—
our house full of aunts and their men

and young Jesuits sent down for the summer.
She laughs as she moves among them, her skirt
swirling like a fern twirled on a stem,

waist as narrow as a girl's again.
My father's eyes follow her across the room.
In the garden, yellow pansies

nod in porch light. Their marker stabbed
in fresh-turned earth
reads "O Suzanna."

Am I the only one who hears
when she sits on the step alone
sucking on the rough, intoxicating

rock bottom of desperation,
each sob buried
in the ratchet of the August dry-birds?

Poise

My mother insists on shoulders straight
and no arms swung while walking.
She requires the lower registers for spoken words
and fewer decibels for the girls than for our brothers.

So, on the night we go together to
the Ladies' Club for Cultural Development
and watch a movie in which snow
falls in a forest to the sound of wind
and the drawn out breath of violins

I use my quiet voice, the soles of my galoshes
flat on the floor, as I point out the metaphor
of hiddenness and revelation made
of having all the trees left bare on one side
while the other sides are coated thickly,
how sunshine pouring between long tree shadows
after the storm shows us that truth
will cut through darkness.

Tsks and gasps do a little dance
around the room as one by one
the ladies' shoulders slump
in the way I know my mother disapproves of.

She stares at them
and then at me,
the only child among the grownups,
as if she's just remembered I am there.

Speaking of The Dead

At the slumber party we ask the Ouija
board who's there. Get the letter *F*,

then, *Soon*. We discuss what happens,
after dying. One girl insists that in the coffin

hair and nails still grow. We scare ourselves
describing what we'll look like then.

Except Maureen, who sits across the room,
robe wrapped tight, chin rigid.

And suddenly
someone whispers

about her mother, and one by one
we try to imagine how that feels.

My Mother Breaks Her Arm Sliding Down the Stairs on A Mattress

How did you break your arm Mrs. English?
Sliding down the stairs.

Did someone push you?
All my daughters.

Was there an argument?
Yes, about who'd go first.

Why did they push you Mrs. English?
I told them they could.

Why would you let them push you down the stairs?
I got to fly. I got to scream like a girl at Godzilla!

The Lady from the Choir Says,
Your Mother Was A Saint

1.
You see how I've had to imagine you—
tried to make my vision fit?
I've re-dreamed your dreams as my own, said

we had this kind of conversation, sat down
and poured over our shared life like tea leaves—
asked for a sign.

I want a mirror that cannot crack.

2.
I loved days when the church was empty.
Loved that Station of the Cross
where Mary weeps beside the Magdalene—

the two of them
like the split trunk of a birch,
bent in different ways but

inseparable.
I loved that the death
was finally done, grief

a resting place.

3.
Ken and I are in Montana.
Smoke from the Crazies rises above the peaks—
an umbilical twist of ash collapsing

in eye-blue skies. There is a hole
in one mountain; a small crater
filled with snow—even now in August.

We stand pink rubber hoppers on green water,
watch for rainbows suspended under mossy logs.
Now and then I see my face in Ken's dark glasses,

a halo of smoke and mountains around my head.

The Space In Between

I tell myself the crows
broke the bird bath
or the gale
or snow
and now a terracotta stream of debris
glazed with cream and verdigris
flows around black wands of dead astilbe,
withered bluebells,
a cracked calligraphy of vinca.

Sometimes we forget,
as we dunk tips of bear claws in coffee,
that we ever drove each other crazy with our grief
and whose turn it is to give. Unlike our mothers,

who were born wanting and died of it,
the birds seem not to miss the bird bath.
If I scatter seed they come.
If the bowl is gone there is other water.

The Blessing

The night my father kissed my brother Pat
on the neck it was summer
and the crescent moon had already set
and we were sitting up late on the patio
singing—something from Carousel,
maybe "Mr. Snow," maybe
"If I Loved You."

And a car rolled in the driveway,
headlights dark, engine cut.
And my father flew out of his chair
and ran down the path,
so we ran too.

And there was Pat in his Navy Blues,
cap flat on his head,
home from Saginaw.
And our father came up behind him
arms open to take him in,
and he kissed the only part of our brother
he could reach that way, the nape of his neck.
He kissed him.

And then it was over and years would pass
and they would leave this earth
without another touch between them.

But I carry them the way they were
that night—father kissing son,
son leaning in
to take the blessing.

Keeping Up

Sometimes it's wind yanking my coat open to the cold
and sometimes it's my husband's hand
on my hip early in the morning, asking.

And sometimes it's just that I wasn't prepared
for something. For instance I didn't know
to study the garden for vole tracks in midwinter
to know where I would not see lilies in the spring.

Sometimes I go to sleep intending to dream
and wake up in the dark instead,
my brother's name beating on my heart
as if it were a mallet and I the drum,

because all I can give is hope
and he's doing what the doctors tell him.

Sometimes I think I'll rototill the garden in April
but that summer I don't get
to the planting.

March 3, 1991

At the undertaker's I open the box,
pull pins from cuffs and collar,
shake out the folds, stroke the soft sleeve
of the nicest shirt my father will ever own.
Then, like the aproned women in *The Gleaners*,
I bow with my sisters over his pockets' leavings.

White comb gray with oil.
Timex with replacement strap.
Cracked wallet—eleven dollars, club IDs,
and the last license issued to our mother
carried all these years behind his own.

She gazes there, as if gazing in,
as if not gazing—
says she was ready, even then;
the high window an idea just forming.

I Imagine My Father Tries His Hand at Memoir

I loved words.

Given the right circumstance I would have been the writer
of my marriage
because I *felt* the language.
When a passenger climbed aboard my bus in winter
 I could see that she was perished with the cold.

For my wife words were building blocks
for sentiments,
rhymes, etcetera. People loved her cards
and her gorgeous cursive…

and it was only when she fell into the abyss, her
manipulations slipped
like a silk scarf grabbed by the wind
and taken out of sight before the owner

even knows it happened. Then,
at least she tried to say it
in her journal…plain words: *I wonder what kind of car he'll buy
with the life insurance claim….*

She wanted me to hold her
but I wouldn't.
I was seeing someone on the side.
I told my girls
I never thought I wouldn't go first.

Blue Swans

Low sun, almost navy sky
stains their great curved bodies,
feet buried in muck,
the space between bellies and water
indigo shadows.
Like Eliot's roses they have the look
of swans that have been looked at—
imagined whole, a filled silence.

A home movie shows me at six,
sliding down the neck of a wooly burro
into my father's arms,
and him returning me to solid ground in one long swing,
the corners of his eyes narrowed in sunlight,
the clickety-click of film in the projector
our only voice.

Each swan lifts one webbed foot
and then the other—stropping
the flats with a faint *thuck*.
When we pass again, I feel how they stir
the sound of us into the mud.

It's been twenty years since I've seen my father's
blue eyes see me. But yesterday I understood,
we carry all that being seen inside us—
it's what calls us to the looking back.

We Start With What We're Given

We read the play in wilted rooms where Venetians clack
as lifted sashes siphon Spring into the gloom.
The boys, whose voices crack,
mumble music they cannot hear,
while the girls recite their lines half in defiance
                                    half in fear.

Sister Helen Joseph stops us
at each archaic or unfamiliar word,
so our pace becomes the pace
of patients in an ethered world.

One week later, under clouds
the shape and shade of unwashed lambs
we ride in a parade of yellow buses to see the film version.
So odd to fill the faded velvet seats at noon
and sit in solid dark all afternoon.
Balcony off limits, girl- and boy-friends kept apart,
we watch as Zefirelli breaks our hearts.

It is the nightingale, says Juliet
as she wakes to shadowed dawn.
But we know it is the morning's lark.
Although if tested, we could not describe its song,
since we've never heard a bird *herald* the day,
still we know, Romeo must go away.

It is the nightingale, cries Juliet, her voice pitched with despair.
Her pale breasts rise like moons through the veil of her dark hair.
And Romeo, who is turned from us as from his one night's wife,
pauses to listen, and doing so, gives us his slender back,
a length of thigh, the curve and cleft of buttocks bared.

All in our rows, as the projector's light plays over each one's gaze
we stare, at what, of one another we have only dreamed 'til then.
We mark the loveliness of lovers in that dark.

And this becomes our tale of Romeo and Juliet—
this crush of flesh and grief
as they cling to one another on the bed, then part
not knowing when they'll meet
again. And though we know, we hope that now,
somehow,
because he's forced their beauty on us like a draught
that wakes us from our childish sleep,

Zefirelli will revise the end—
take back the lark.

Song

Upstairs my husband plays a riff in a minor key
which I once explained to my students is
the key of sorrows, but also reverie.

Under glowing nimbus clouds
an osprey rises in widening swirls
above the little pond stocked with rainbows.

All day we have stayed at home.
No business to take us further than the barn.
Contrails of East-bound planes
thin to gauzy ribbons.

It's not that we don't care to travel,
but sometimes we can't think
of where to go or why to leave
home. Even so,
I've been remembering

blonde meadows sprawled
beside the Adriatic—
the scatter
rug we found beside the road, fringe
half torn away, its pattern obscured
by a blanket of the olive blossoms
that drifted everywhere on the wind.

Upstairs, the click of case clasps—
footfall on the stairs.

Woolgathering

I pick up the sound of a motorcycle on a dirt road;
jazz piano in a room just going dark in April;
that final
loving letting go—
and I card the wool.

II

A line is not really important because it records what you have seen, but because it will lead you on to see.

John Berger, *On Seeing*

Translating Rilke In Winter

At Brewer's Marina
I prowl in open sheds
under keels and hulls
scraped clean of barnacles and
mussel beard. Each bilge hole
hums like an empty moon shell.

Last night, in "Einsamkeit"
I found the word *switterstunden*,
which Snow resolves
as the hours in between,
but which I call
the hermaphroditic hours.

Because what's more likely
in a poem about loneliness,
that meditates on what it means
to wake up in the wrong bed?

If I had not been to sea
I wouldn't understand these boats in cradles.
If I had not wanted in the night
I would not know this heart
braced in its caul of ribs.

Lesson 1—Action

Let the cloud colors out in long furls
of lilac, tangerine, and ash,
so the sky appears to be escaping the frame.
Let the jib curl
like a fat white apostrophe
above the beat-flat bow turned east.

Clutter the horizon with crests and troughs
and sea foam flung skyward.
Let the gulls trail green kelp in their bills
and their orange feet drag behind them.

Make the girls' screams as bright and solid
as the stones they skip across the water,
one, two, three,   eleven!

Let the horse-head seal on his rock
resist the brain's instruction to flee
as charcoal fins pierce the water.

Picasso's Women

We feel the way the wooden frame
stretches them almost to tearing,

arms and legs and eyes
where they shouldn't be,

art when there was nothing else
left.

My daughter hates him for this
dismantling. She believes in wholeness

as if it were a grace we all can muster—
that we do not give ourselves in pieces,

but like the shed skin of the green snake
she discovered in the garden, almost whole,

still shaped like itself,
its stripes now draped across her table.

Upon Discovering the Task Is Larger Than First Predicted

Renunciation is a strange word—
the taking back of previous approvals,
previous beliefs or trusts

or love. I wasn't ready to go there.
The field of endeavor was not yet dry
of my blood.

But I could hear the young coyote
on his own in the dark,
scrape the air with his need.

I could hear him hesitate—try again,
not give in to the silence
that met his howling.

When it's time to go
I will walk away. Like the night
around that coyote, I will not call back.

This is a poem

for all the men
who walked away—

who left me standing under apple trees
in winter starlight or summer's sulk,

who sat in my father's house wanting but not touching
me, our knees grazing beneath the kitchen table.

This is for the men who knew they didn't know
how to listen, who stared when I used words

like transcendence, who offered gifts of raucous
music. This is for the men who kissed

me as if kissing their mothers on the cheek
and the ones who tongued me deeply,

their hands roaming my body
like a closed door in the dark.

This is for their faith in their wanting,
for the lines they drew in me like the ancients

who mapped rivers
in the spaces between the stars.

Lesson 2—On Time and Desire

In a house on the bluff a dog's shut in
and barking. We can hear him from the beach
between the waves' breaking. He thinks

he's been left too long. *Come back.*
Come back, he repeats,
as if his bark will conjure

the key in the lock.
We can hear his yearning.
Then, the barking stops.

Which is not the same as ends.
It's just the dog has no fixed
calculus for how to get what's wanted.

When he remembers his need he'll start
again. He'll ask and ask and ask—

I Imagine My Father Tries His Hand
at Memoir, Again

I am imagining my father sitting down to write his memoir;
how he would face the blank page, the crowd of sounds
and images competing to be the first note
of what swirls inside him—

the creak of the horse-drawn wagon on Hyde Park Avenue,
from which, corner after corner he threw
bundles of papers to the Sunday newsboys, or the roar
of the paper mill on second shift, still in his head while he slept

or the tat-tat-tat of bullets ripping the water around him
as he waded toward the beach at Tarawa, Browning
high over his head, his partner, Jake, ankle deep ahead,
crate of rounds shouldered, when the unhearable
shot slams into Jake's chest, and my father must rescue
the ammunition,

the shallow breath of his wife in her first labor,
the little box he holds in his lap two years later,
the jokes he tells in tough times all swallowed
by the small neat hole dug for his daughter,
filled with noon light beside her grandfather's grave,

his screams filling the frowsy cups of mauve tea roses
on the wallpaper of their bedroom that final go round with Malaria,
kids sent out to play while his wife calls his name,
trying to convince him, *this is not Peleliu or Guadalcanal.
You're not in the hospital in Brisbane,*

the crack of a stick on the jungle floor that flies out of the pot
as my mother snaps dry pasta into boiling water—

his father's roar as he attempts the steps to the second floor
and tumbles backwards, calling *Maude! Maudie, get down here*

and help me damn you! Thwack of the stickball bat
against the fence or the belt against his legs,
another night another rage—Frankie's sass at supper,
the sound of his chair shoved back so fast it flips
on the brick patterned linoleum and Frankie is hanging
by his ankles from our father's hands, the silence
spreading inside us as our father bellows, *You. Will. Not. Talk.
Back.* Frankie flying up and down like a pump's handle,
our mother calling, *Lester. Lester*. But not touching him,
not grabbing her son from his father's grasp.
I imagine the blank paper an enemy, the way his
hold on the now might fly apart, if just once the words
were brought to ink—the genii pushed out of the bottle,
the bottle so crammed with the unsaid the genii is almost
not breathing, almost dead, and my father's unconscious thought
that it must not be allowed to

live. It's my father's hundredth birthday and I'm still looking,
still convinced there was more to know than this.

So I give him this day, the electric green of the fields after rain,
where deer graze at dusk, their fawns hidden in the uncut hay,
I give days of chilly sun and rolling cumulus, Venus fading
in the morning blue, the chuckle of wood ducks in vernal pools,
the first whip-o-wills calling in Spring dark—I give him the sorrow
of Homs because now he can take it and maybe even weep,
and the sweetness of his great-grandkids,
their blooming, chortles, and silly laughs,
born late enough to know him only as we share him.

I give the poems I keep writing like rough maps
of the world, berms of language I have made
to protect me for a moment at a time
from the violence of being human—

words to root what love is,
hardy, green, and tender as April's grass.

Shell Life

Listen,
when a snail dies its home
fills with sea sound. Hold it
to your ear all day
you won't hear a single word
of grief.

Poem

A wasp bobbles in the seam
where wall meets eave,
batters the salt smudged glass,
striving, always, out.

A percussionist,
it tests each vertical for egress,
thumps the bodhran on my shelf,
red grain of my corner cupboard.

The sun westers.
The room cools.

Still my prisoner,
it ornaments a swell of curtain,
cellophane wings shut,
stinger curved under itself.

It can't remember how it got in.
I can't touch it to let it out.

When You Ask Again

From the dunes, Penikese
seems to drift on the horizon.
Its dot of barracks empty,

barns and sheepfold shut
it hasn't seen
a sheep or prisoner in a century.

We square our hands to frame the view.
Beach plums by the bathhouse drop
and split in rippling heat.

Two egrets dip at fish
in the estuary's trickle.
The tide will not turn for hours.

I am the woman you shouldn't marry.

Why We Need Salt

All morning I use my body like a tool,
heave my weight onto the step of the spade,
then cut in and under the garden's edge.

Little toads the color of old milk chocolate pop
from clods of earth. Worms wriggle away from themselves
sliced in two by my shovel blade.

Asparagus tips break the surface,
red, urgent. I lay out the string
that tells my brother where to till

and what he should not disturb.
Last night I saw my first image from inside—
buildings broken open by shell fire,

a river of people flowed down the boulevard,
their progress slowed by the silt of nowhere to go.
Refugees with no refuge.

What lodged deepest was their silence—
the sense that there are no words
for this stranding in a world that does not see them.

Preparing lunch I listened
to my body's hunger. Watched my hands
slice and fan the meat across the plate,

satisfied my mouth with salt
on cucumber and cabbage. God
is not in the event, but in our response.

Bread—1

*Young girls who had 'friends' among the male inmates and who used to get gifts of food, asked me to draw their portraits. The payment—
a piece of bread.*

                                                          Esther Lurie

On Saturdays I gather the week's stale
slices, dip them in milk and egg sprinkled
with cinnamon and sugar, fry them in butter.

I warm the maple syrup so it will saturate
the gold brown crust,
pour small glasses of juice at the table.

The house fills with the smell of bread and coffee.
The scrape of forks on ironstone
our only shared sound—the sticky spot

he leaves the only guarantee
that we were both at table
once the plates are cleared.

This is the price
I tell myself—the cost
I cannot quite believe,

the memory of what I used to wish for
a soft amber drop
I sponge away before it hardens.

Lesson 3—Distance

A white-necked magpie floats overhead.

One sense of distance can be achieved
by two lines drawn diagonally, if
as they move across the page, the space between them
diminishes to a thread.
This will lead the eye deep
into the field or to the stone walls
that frame the groves, or the green
shadows where, now,
the magpie mutters
like a priest in his confessional.
Who does not need
forgiveness?

The instructor demonstrates how horizontal lines
drawn parallel, define what's near
and what the eye might imagine
by bending light—here, the threshold of my door,
there, East of everything,
the Adriatic where an orange smear signals morning,
the bream and mackerel boats heading out,
their engines' putter blessing
the hammered silver day.

I follow as she explains how each
vertical construction infers sky,
raised cross, soaring bird, any form
that climbs above mid-page will raise the eye.
The priest-bird overhead, clouds above him,
empty space filling in around his long, slow glide.

I want to see what the bird sees—to float
on wood and taffeta
like the locksmith of Sablé, but
I am anchored here—mid-life, mid-page.
Tomorrow,
wind.

Morning Prayer

Bless the grey weight of early morning—
the plain of clouds
over the soft lead of the kettle-holes
along the lower road.

Bless each pond's horizontal totem—
pitch pine or scrub oak, their dozen arms plunged
in water, as if searching for a dropped key
that will unlock summer.

Bless the pond with the pussy-willow fringe
whose thousand gold-green thumbs
have bamboozled the moon
into hanging until morning.

Bless the sun
still tangled in the woods.
May it find its way into the blue.

III

In Esther Lurie's view, every artist in the Ghetto [was] obliged to immortalize—each according to his ability and technique—every aspect of the Ghetto reality. General, large-scale events will remain in people's memory. But singular episodes such as the sufferings of an individual are bound to be forgotten.

Avraham Tory, *Surviving the Holocaust: The Kovno Ghetto Diary*

Kovno, 1939

Please send buttons—
aqua to remind me of the sea
or pewter for Tel Aviv's sky in winter.
Send the leather green of lemon leaves

or red clay that has paled to pink
like the tracks in the road where the butcher's
cart has lumbered toward the market

its leaking lade staining the dust.

Send me one pearl as small as a baby's tooth,
from the dozen that marched up your spine
on your wedding morning, or black

like the beads in father's cuffs. If you can find it,
send the clasp of matched olive burls
I used to twine through the wool of my shawl

on those mornings when we hunched against the cold
as we carried home the day's bread, the silky steam
of morning's milk mixed with our own breath.

I promise I will bring them when I return.

Notes on "Girl with Yellow Star"

They wear stars
on their backs, off center bulls'
-eyes, and on their hearts—

children too. All Jews,
all made of dirt and eyes and hiding
behind eyes that do not see

as they cross the wooden bridge over Aryan street
so as not to mix their mud
with purer street filth—

the messenger boy wears his uniform,
its bright star part
of how the people know who is coming,

and the garden girls, barefoot in the rows,
their matched twirling
as they chase out the gold

finches who tear the tender leaves of seedlings.

Later, fire will engulf the frail
and the hiders. The walls and floors,
the bridge, the open ghetto gate

will disappear like stars at daybreak,
earth and clay the only things
that do not burn.

Kovno Ghetto, July 1941

She misses the sky above the sea
where frigate birds drift
like veils dragged on breezes,

the sloth-slow sun of midday,
shutters closed against the heat
contented bubbehs snoring,

the soft slap of soles
against the cobbles of neve Tzdedek
and the din of pigeons
on the tin roofs over the fruit stalls,

the distant shriek
of freighters' horns as they leave the harbor,
the waves, beaten silver by the sun.
She misses her sisters in summer dresses

when all were young, braids bouncing
as they chased the iceman for a chunk
to slide along their arms, dripping cool
in the unrelenting heat.

She misses her mouth filled with breath
to blow charcoal dust from the paper on her table
where dancers' arms are raised,
toes en pointe on a stage.

All across the ghetto the day
has sidled down the walls as shadows rise.
              Her hands
merge with the dark.

Visitation

She crawls up onto my bed
and tucks herself behind my bent knees.
We cannot separate.

A thin broth of moonlight caught in the trees
spreads across the garden brush
so one side of every stick
shimmers while the other sides melt
into one another, a mass grave
of cherry, pear, and pine.

It's 3 in the morning when she shifts
to sit on my Book of Windows, between
my glass of water and blue lamp.
She stares at me
as if I were her mother dreaming,

or a fever lingered in my bones, but
she does not sing to me or stroke my ear
the way my own mother did when I was small
and facing down some shadow demon.

She is only here because I spoke her name
today, so she was conjured,
her eyes faint as this night's sky.
Her pinched fingers flick at the empty space—
inscribe a scrap of linen only she can see.

I turn my back and feel her shift again,
curled against my hip. I know
she is not sleeping.
It's a way of being and not being

she learned in the stifle of Stutthof—

how to be unseen while seeing,
how to lay your hope in a coffin
and pretend it is a bed,
how to ink the prisoners' numbers
back into legibility—
make the unseeable
seen.

I want to tell her, *It isn't a sin to sleep.*
The mind will not punish the body in dreams.
The body will find its own way.
The dim, blister moon will fade in daylight.

I would stroke her foot if I could reach it.
I would pull it against my ribs
the way my mother warmed my own feet
when I had skated too long on Rabbit Pond.
Rubbing the blood back into circulation
she'd say the itch and sting were good signs.

Tonight I am awake with Esther.
My hands are open and warm.
And she is considering what it would mean
to close her eyes and rest, if I will promise
to keep my own eyes open until morning.

Kovno Ghetto, November 1941

She chooses an attic window for her frame,
her eye finds the place on the page

that will center the orphaned chimney stack.
As the ink finds its way to the nib

silence
absorbs the memory of sounds;

lock's click,
splash of kerosene,

screams of terror,
screams of agony.

Lines crawl onto her page,
sprawl—

a great dispossession
of what the mind cannot unknow.

All afternoon she sits.
Cross-hatched slashes of ink

capture the collapsed roof,
fill in the solid black

of the single, sagging rafter,
shattered glass caught in sunlight

like stars that prick the winter sky.
Too far away to see their ashes,

but still too close,
she focuses.

Lines crawl onto her page,
sprawl toward the edges of her frame,

tangle now and then—close up the field,
smear

when her ink thickens in the cold.

Plymouth, October 2016

In the tumble of the Reserverat's yard
unhoused belongings made
a forest of furniture,
rags for tree leaves,
brambles made of bed springs
and bits of bicycles.

And in the pottery, a pair of urns
left half-turned on the wheel
as the Great Aktion requires
everyone in the Square—
the sheen of damp clay
fading as the SS officer at his table
points left or right, and the Jewish police
hide this or that already counted person
in the crowd.

Think of the well chosen line
and the situation of its choosing—
does art save in the moment
from the moment?
And what survives?

Kovno Ghetto, March 1942, Imagining Mamma's Birthday

While the sun still sleeps she'll go to the kitchen.
She'll be thinking about what it means
to wake in a house minus daughters,
in a city where the limestone walls
are washed orange to gilt
and later, a red that fades to sepia—
which is when the scent of the trees in bloom
presses against her skin
like a fever only a glass of tea can undo.

She will eat the small honey cake
her husband brings her. He will say,
Because we can Bluma. Because they are with us.
They are smiling. They are weeping for joy
over you, telling stories
of the hoopoe and the honey bee,
of Vashti and the Jew.
They are going to sleep side by side,
dreaming of your fingers braiding the dough—
how the bread will send a fragrant steam
into the air,
a cloud so rich
it could be eaten.

Kovno Ghetto, April 1942, Portrait Before Shabbat

Smoke is difficult,
its shapes amorphous
and un-durable. Ash
is more predictable,
able to hurl itself into a place and stay there.

With the wind's help
it will sift its way down
to melt and stain the pocked ice
or shrivel on the wet Spring grass
or land on some edge fine as a blade
against the neck
just below the jawline.

She has watched the elders pull their beards
taut in contemplation, as if the sun, by rising,
had licked the morning clean—and the mud
that shone between the rows of cabbages
were the glow of Jerusalem.
Her pentimento mingles shame
with resistance—

And who will walk into the holy city?

Kovno Quotidian

Like her neighbors
she completes each task given.

Turn the lathe in the munitions plant.
Ignore your hunger.

Paint the orphaned chimney of the hospital
the Gestapo set aflame.

Include the cinder clouded slush of orphans'
remains. Hang a show of photographs

and sketches and invite answers
to the question, What is Jewish

Art? Let go of nothing.
Let go of everything.

Kovno Ghetto, January 1943

In the night, snow
filigreed the cedars
along the road to the Ninth Fort,
hid the frozen mud
beneath a sparkling talc,
and now,
the sun
like a platinum flame,
consumes this world's dark places,
as if each were exalted space—
their forms so bright
the devil would vanish
in the face of Adonai.

Kovno Ghetto, Spring 1943

They hide in the forests,
still Jews.
They lie in the pits of the Ninth Fort,
still Jews.

The same colors they have always been,
the same wings hidden inside their coats,
same guns in pockets
or no guns.

They resist in body or in spirit,
each attempt at capture.
Some are thieves in Jews' clothing,
some prophets, some broken saints.

Some are artists who follow the line
across the page like a map

or the lines in the feathers
of the raven and the lark,
made for lift and thrust,
each bird the color of its world,

gold sun, iridescent night—mud
brown, blood.

Kovno Ghetto, June 1944

Beside the road that climbs the hill,
green briars sprawl among the cedars
where larks and red-capped sparrows nest.
A woman lifts her head,
lips parted, an unspoken word
on her tongue. Her father's stars
flutter from her pocket.
Yellow finches bathe
in road dust, then flit away.

Kovno Ghetto, July 1944

The SS knew which Jews
would be able to make wings
and the bricks of their own prison—

that in Stutthof typhus would assist
the guards and Kapos
to reduce numbers.

The Elders knew who was and who was
not among the living—who would hide
in the Ghetto thinking,

I have survived Kovno,
now I will live.
Until the fires found them.

Transport, July 1944

What is Stutthof?

It is as far as the eye can see
into the dark.

It is a language
that leaves a track across your mind

so rutted, no one can follow
where it leads.

Plymouth, February 2017

There is no other news of her sister
who died in Auschwitz along with her son—
no name for either, no footnote to explain
why they were in Kovno in the first place—
no brother-in-law, no extended family.
Perhaps her name
was one detail too many for the story.

I have looked and looked for her face
in the sketches of Kovno's inmates,
but only find her in a photograph from Palestine
in which five siblings fill the field with steady gazes,
their parents seated in their midst.

Maybe she's the one taking the photograph
at the beach on the North Sea in 1935,
in which Esther stands, straight-backed, sun-glassed,
smiling directly at the camera, dark curls
lifted off her face by breeze,
or maybe she is the woman with her back
to us, preferring not to be seen.

The day they were driven out of Kovno
in separate directions,
where did Esther hide her sister's name?

Stutthof, 1944, Bread 2

Sawdust mixed in the dough
fills bellies cheaply,
so the factory lines stay full.
When a prisoner drops
where she is standing
and is dragged aside
her mates
think about her portion.
They know it won't nourish
them the way bread should, still, they want it.
That way, maybe a few more days….

They have heard the bombers in the distance.

Leibisch, August 1944, Nummer Schreiberen

Breath blooms in the cold room,
her tongue smacks as she swallows.

Tap of wooden nib on glass rim,
excess ink slips back into the bottle.

She pauses, wrist suspended,
then begins.

The first number on rough linen
is a wren scratching for wood mites,

the second and third
are Spring leaves

unfurling in the wind,
the fourth one weeps

saturates the worn cloth
and stains the table.

With eight, a flash of anguish—
how to face this infinity?

The seven's quiet slash,
the silent open mouth of zed—

fingertips clouded with ink,
she hands each armband to its prisoner.

The doctor's wrist watch ticks.
Two glass syringes lie on a tray

in the sickroom beside two prisoners
unfit for labor.

She hears the bed springs' squeak
and above the camp, the rush of hoopoes,

the black barbs of their wings
beyond number.

Leibisch, October 1944

Open the window and wait.
First you will hear the clatter
of wheels across the bridge,
then the scuff of boots in slush.

Next you will hear your own breathing,
but not until you hear the wheels
and the boots and the breath of others
falling through the slats that make the beds.

You will watch your own breath,
its loaf of air
that dissolves uneaten.
Open the window and wait.

You will see the shapes of sleepers
merged with their shadows, the way
the walls' knots stare
into the dark like spies

who counted your fingers
while you lay sleeping, who count your breaths,
record them with torn retinas that make a silver
flashing beneath your lids—
who decide they will not deport you this time

because your back is needed at the mill
or your hands at the kiln.

Open the window and wait.
The smell of sawed wood will come
and tell you its story of deep summer,

remind you of the groves where lemons'
scent pressed against your skin
like a lover's tongue pressing
past your lips to find you.

The forest where the trees stood
is in the barracks with you now,
in each bunk and floorboard.
Open the window and wait

for the pterodactyl whine of the wireless
across the frozen yard,
where the warm coats with their warm boots
smoke cigarettes, blow rings into blue air,
muttering to one another that this is almost over.

Be ready.
Be quiet.
The fire is coming soon.

Open the window.

Wait.

Tel Aviv, July 1945

Gulls hang silent above the harbor.
The streets beyond the wharf yaw
in the heat.
Soon lines will sprawl again,
drawn out of the acid cuts
of memory—each
strike drawing that world
back into existence.
The past travels with us.

We drop anchor.

Notes:

10-11. All italicized words are from Bartolo Cattafi's poem "Descent To The Throne," in *Winter Fragments: Selected Poems 1945-1979,* Rina Ferrarelli, translator.

22. The reference to "Eliot's roses" refers to lines 27-28 in T.S. Eliot's, "Burnt Norton, Section I" of *Four Quartets:* "… for the roses/ Had the look of flowers that are looked at."

28. "Einsamkeit," by Ranier Maria Rilke, is included in *The Book Of Images*, Edward Snow, translator.

38. Penikese Island is one the Elizabeth Islands in Buzzards Bay off the south coast of Massachusetts. Over the last 2 centuries it has been variously, a sheep farm, a leper hospital, a home for troubled youth, and a prison.

45-67. The poems in Section III rely on details provided in Avraham Tory's, *Surviving The Holocaust: The Kovno Ghetto Diary*, the autobiographical notes of Esther Lurie, as well as her art work, some of which survived the holocaust and other work she produced after she returned to Tel Aviv in 1945.

About the Author

Miriam O'Neal's poems and reviews have appeared in AGNI, Blackbird Journal, Marlboro Review, Ragazine, Solidago Journal, Southern Poetry Journal, and many other journals. She has been a finalist for the Massachusetts Cultural Council Grants in Poetry, and for Louisiana Literature's Tenth Annual Poetry Prize, as well as a Fellow in the Beginning Translators Fellowship Program at the American Literary Translators Association (ALTA) for her translations of Italian poet, Alda Merini. She took her graduate degree at the Writing Seminars Program at Bennington College in Vermont. She lives in Plymouth, Massachusetts.

Made in the USA
Middletown, DE
28 August 2019